Step by Step

How To Draw For Kids

Book 1

1st Edition, 2018

© How To Draw For Kids

All rights reserved.

This book belongs to:

① ② ③ ④ ⑤ ⑥ ⑦ ⑧ ⑨

Here you can practice...

① ② ③

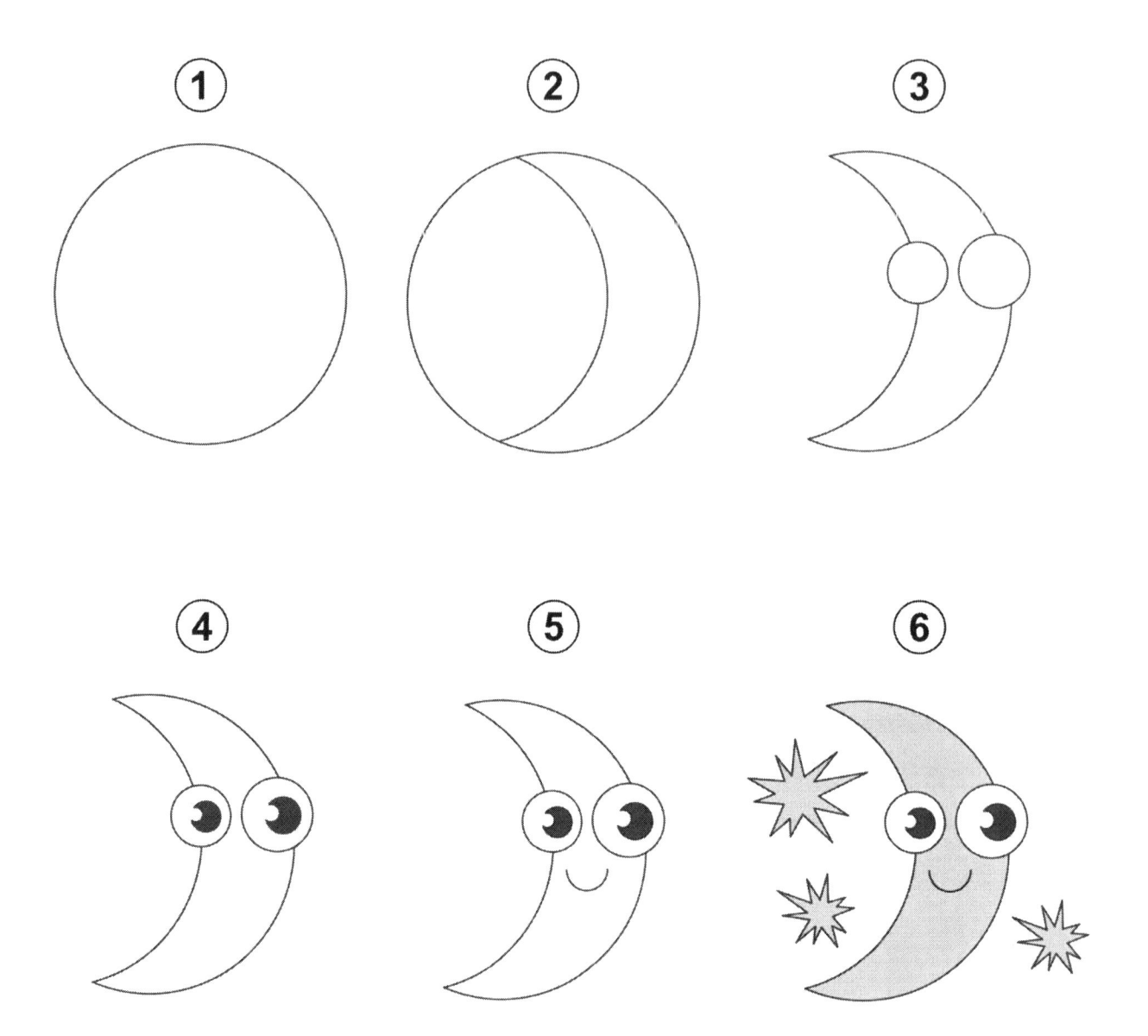

④ ⑤ ⑥

Here you can practice...

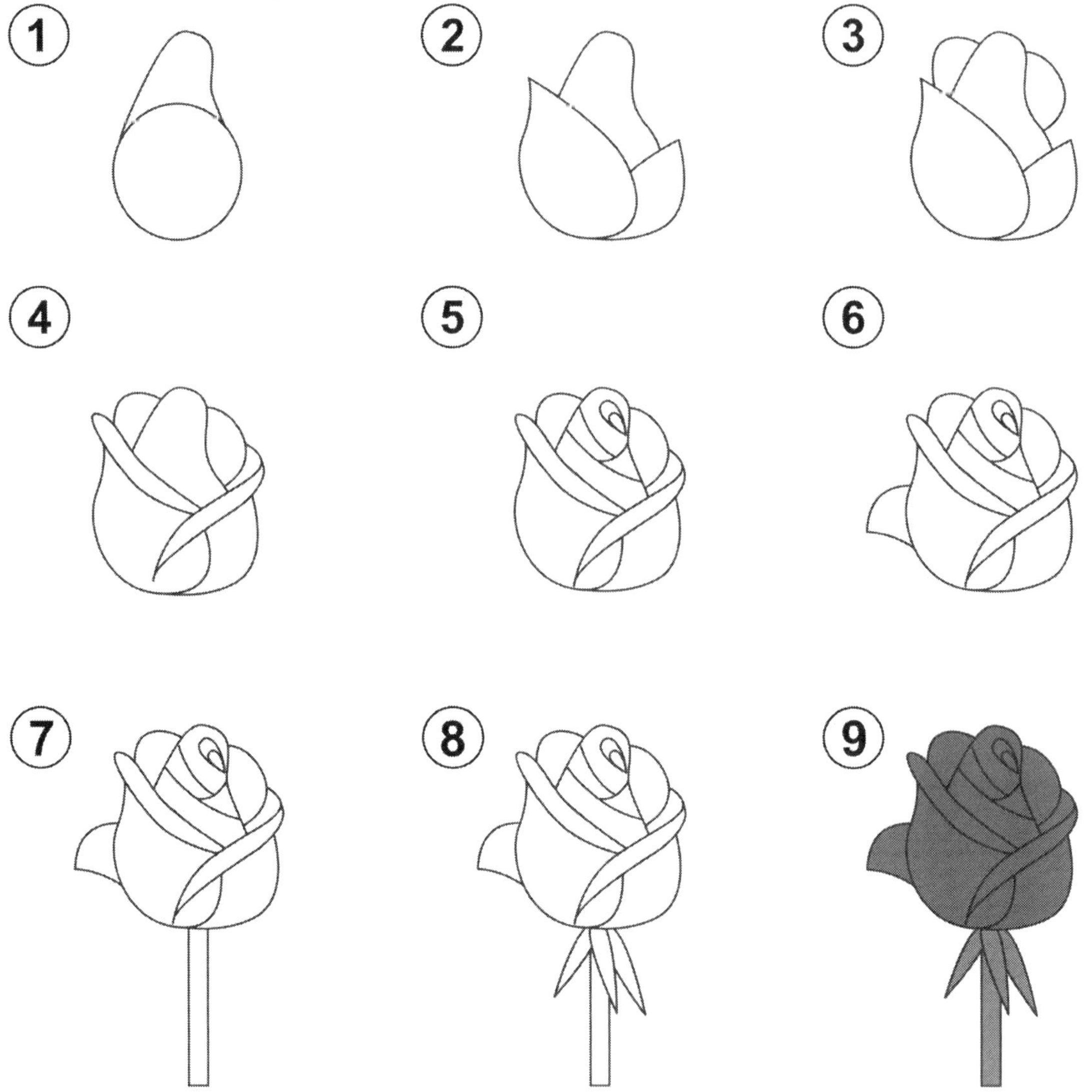
1
2
3
4
5
6
7
8
9

Here you can practice...

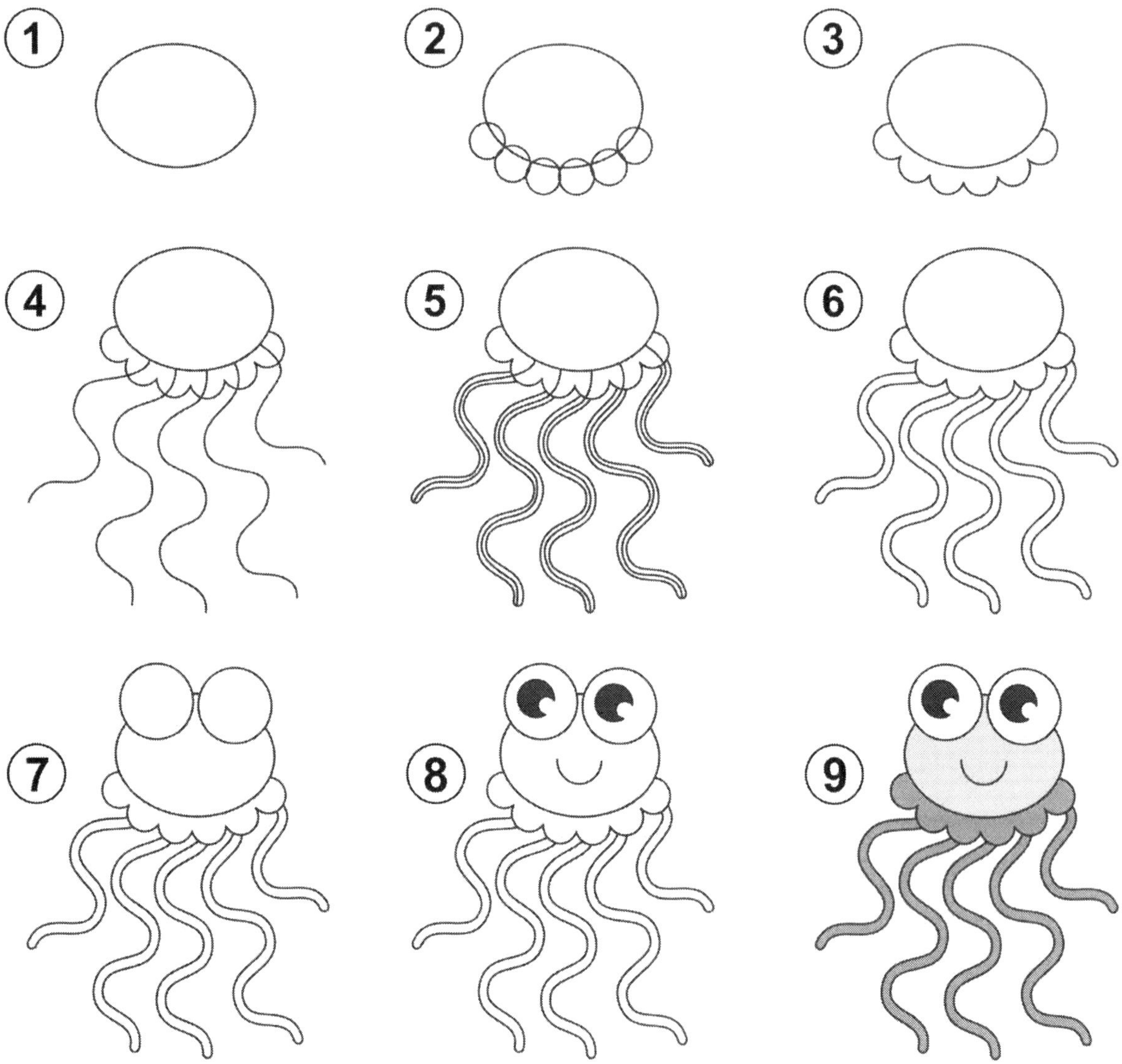
1
2
3
4
5
6
7
8
9

Here you can practice...

① ② ③
④ ⑤ ⑥
⑦ ⑧ ⑨

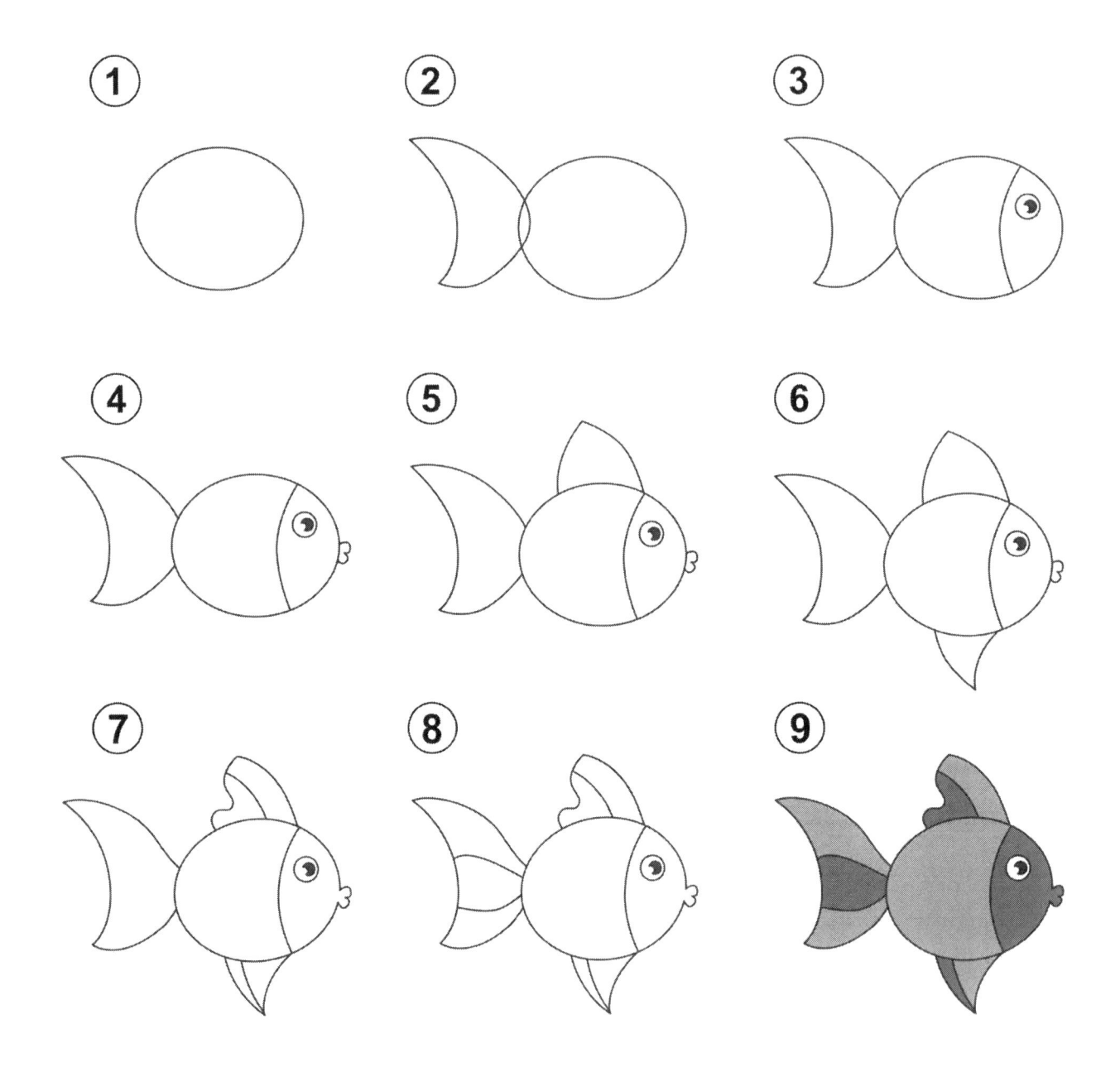

Here you can practice...

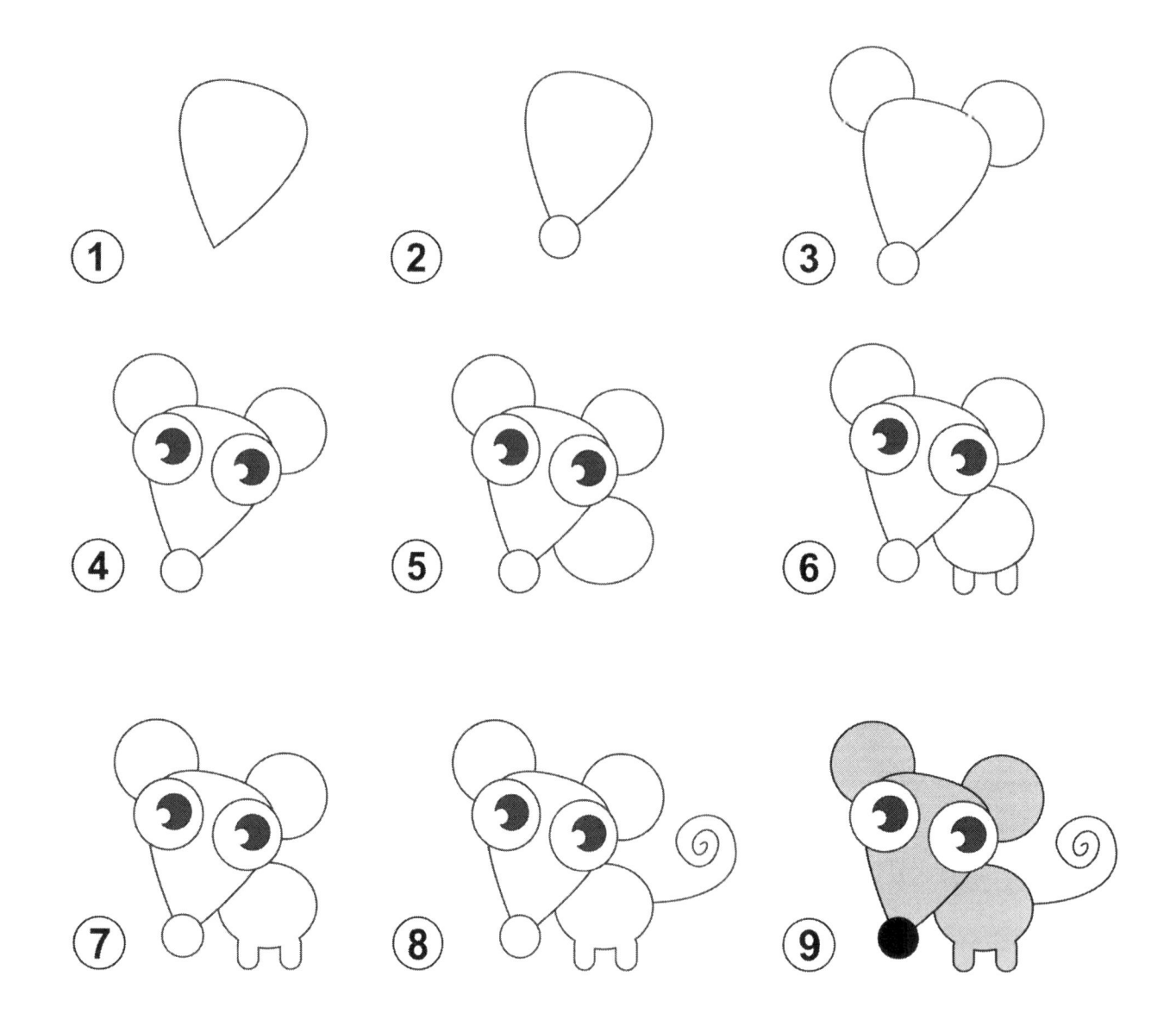

Here you can practice...

① ② ③ ④ ⑤ ⑥ ⑦ ⑧

Here you can practice...

① ② ③ ④ ⑤
⑥ ⑦ ⑧ ⑨
⑩ ⑪ ⑫

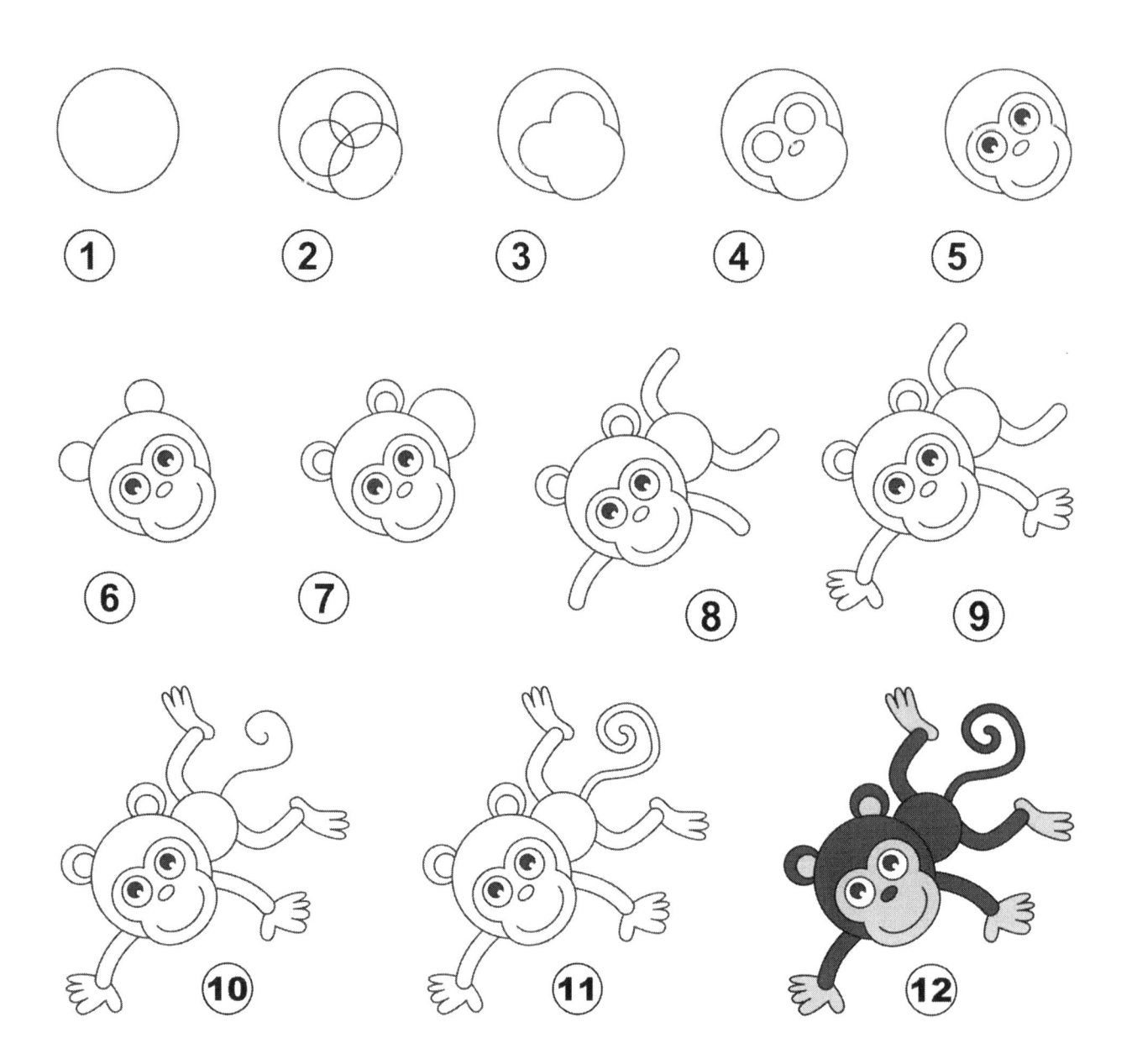

Here you can practice...

① ② ③ ④ ⑤ ⑥ ⑦ ⑧ ⑨

Here you can practice...

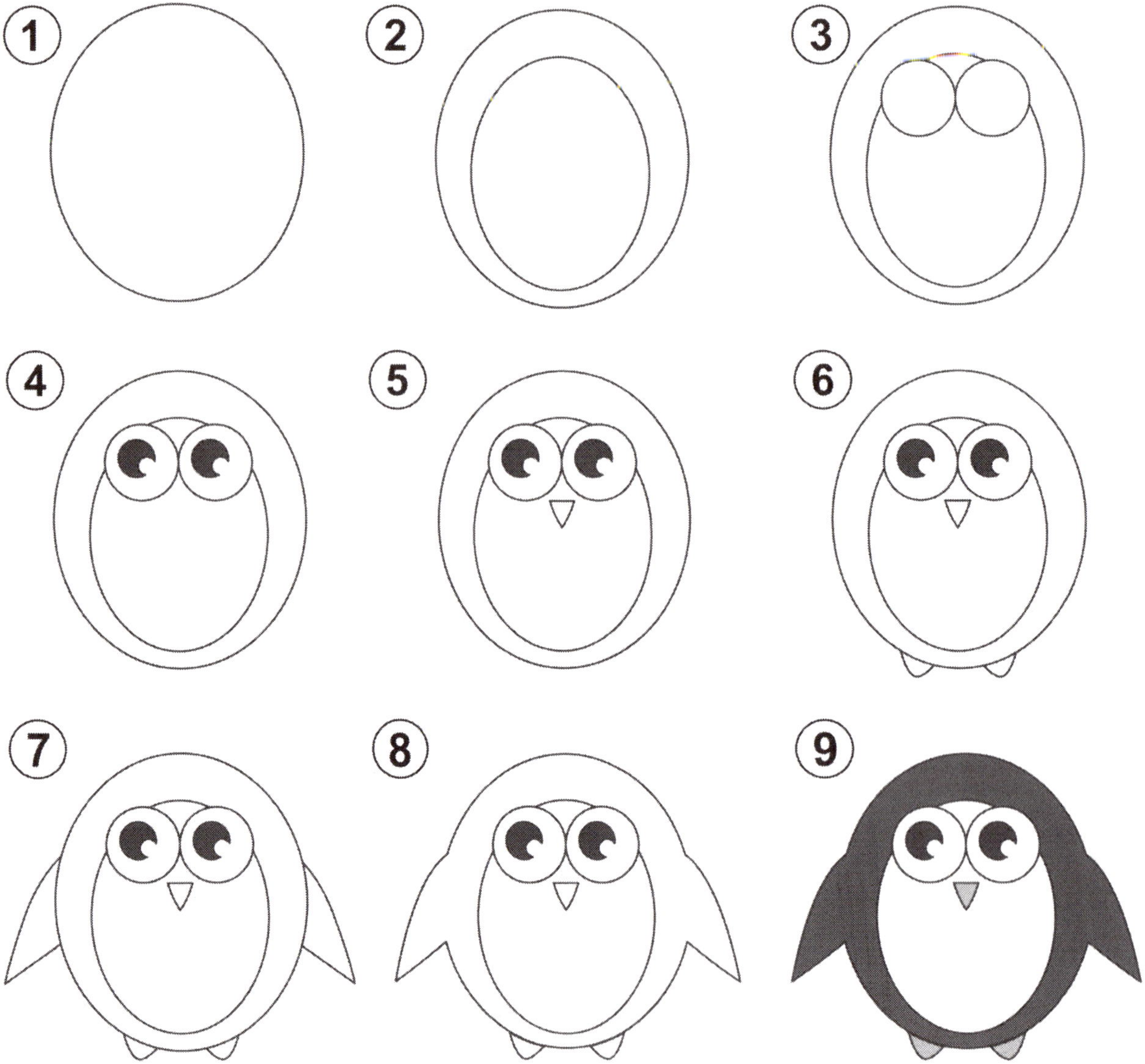
1
2
3
4
5
6
7
8
9

Here you can practice...

① ② ③ ④
⑤ ⑥ ⑦ ⑧
⑨ ⑩ ⑪ ⑫

Here you can practice...

① ② ③ ④ ⑤ ⑥ ⑦ ⑧ ⑨

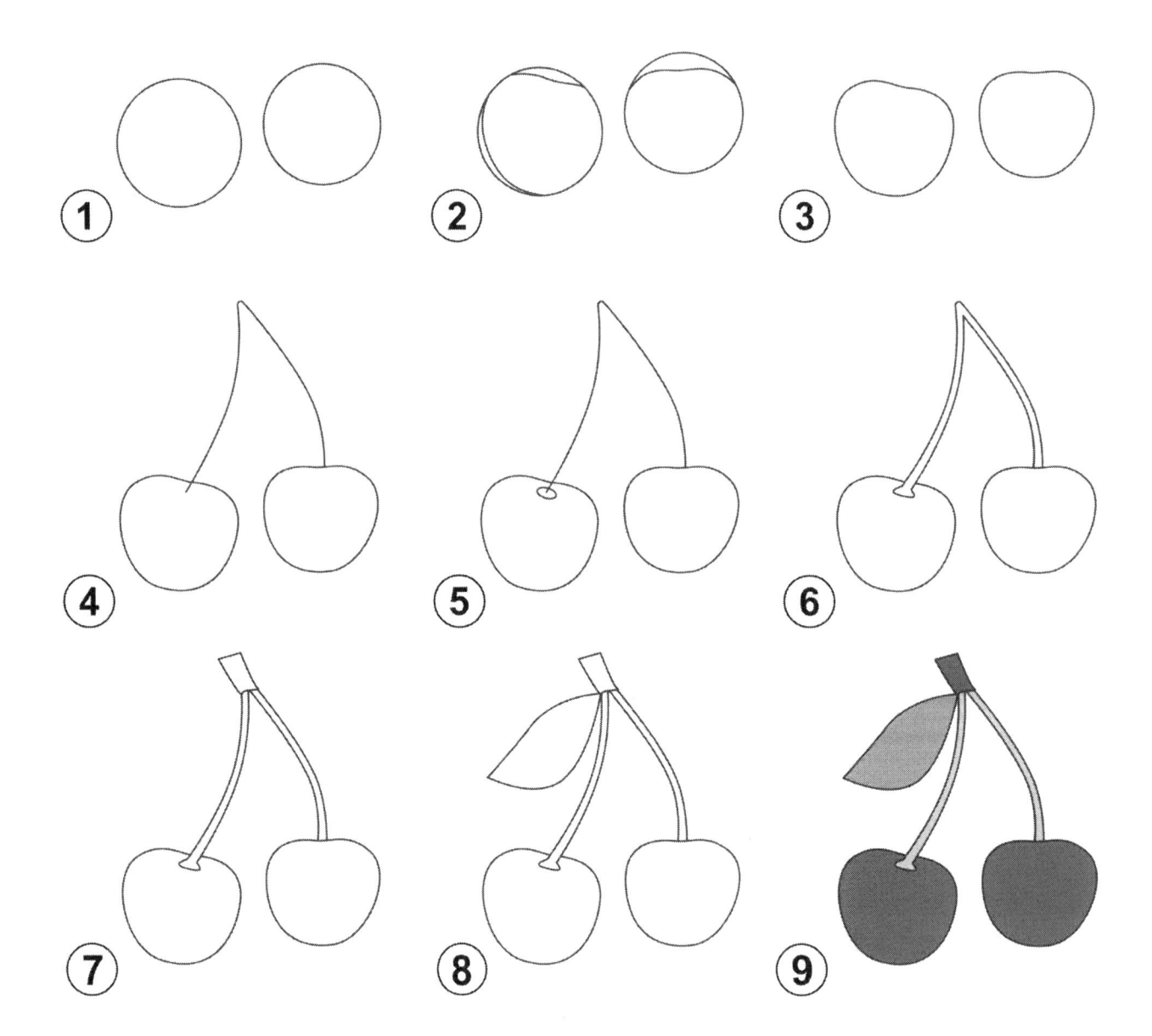

Here you can practice...

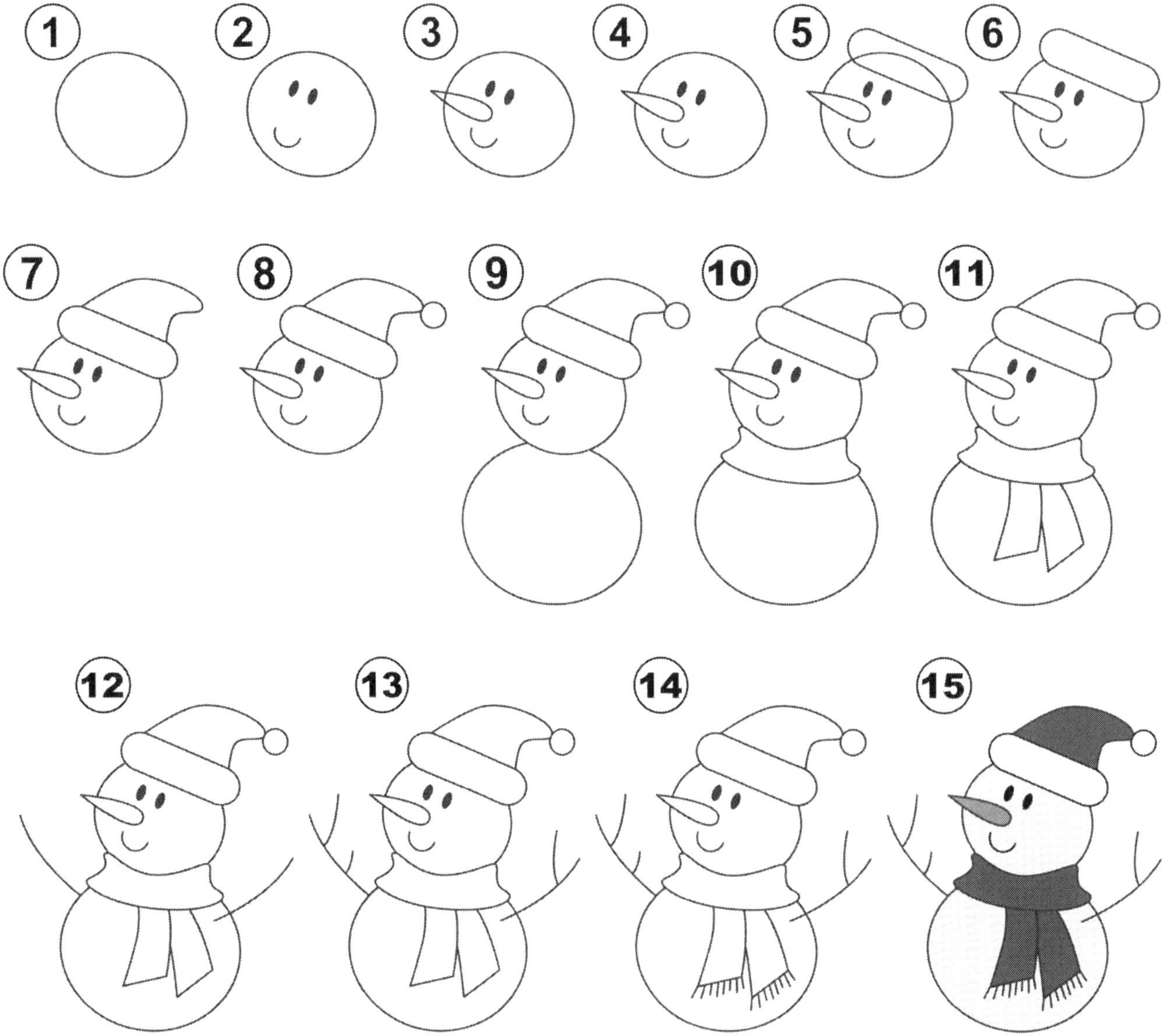
1
2
3
4
5
6
7
8
9
10
11
12
13
14
15

Here you can practice...

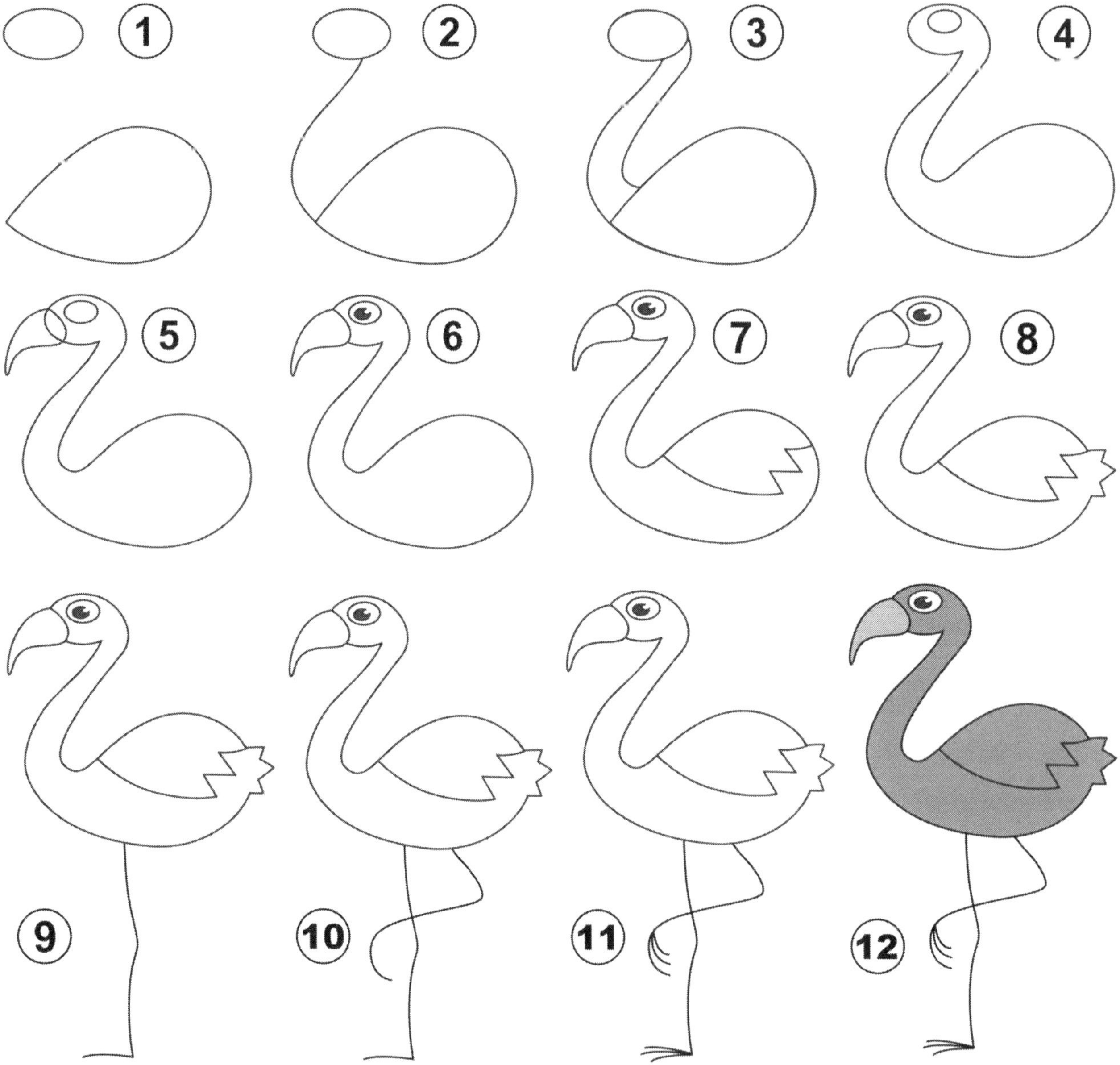
1
2
3
4
5
6
7
8
9
10
11
12

Here you can practice...

① ② ③
④ ⑤ ⑥
⑦ ⑧ ⑨

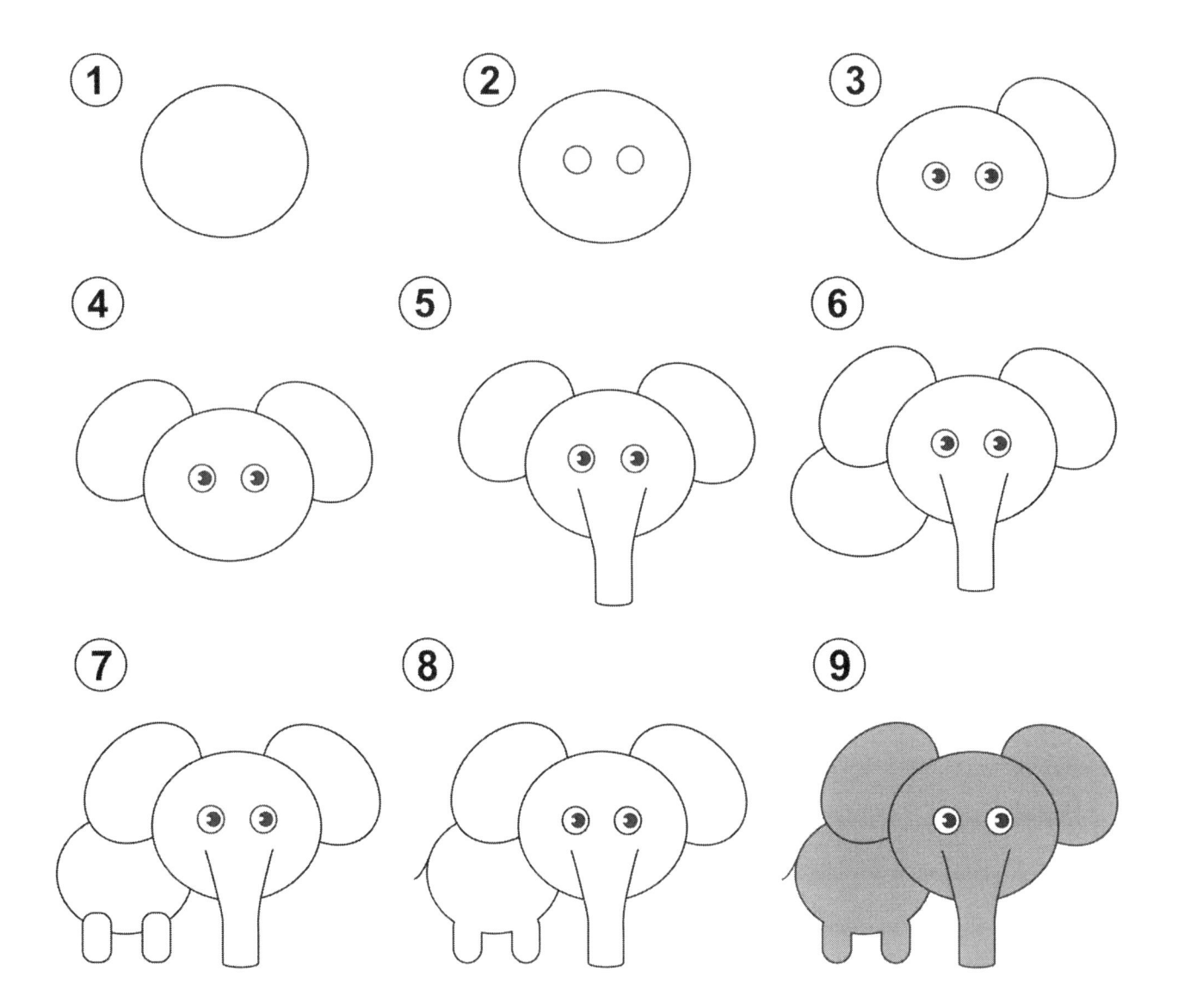

Here you can practice...

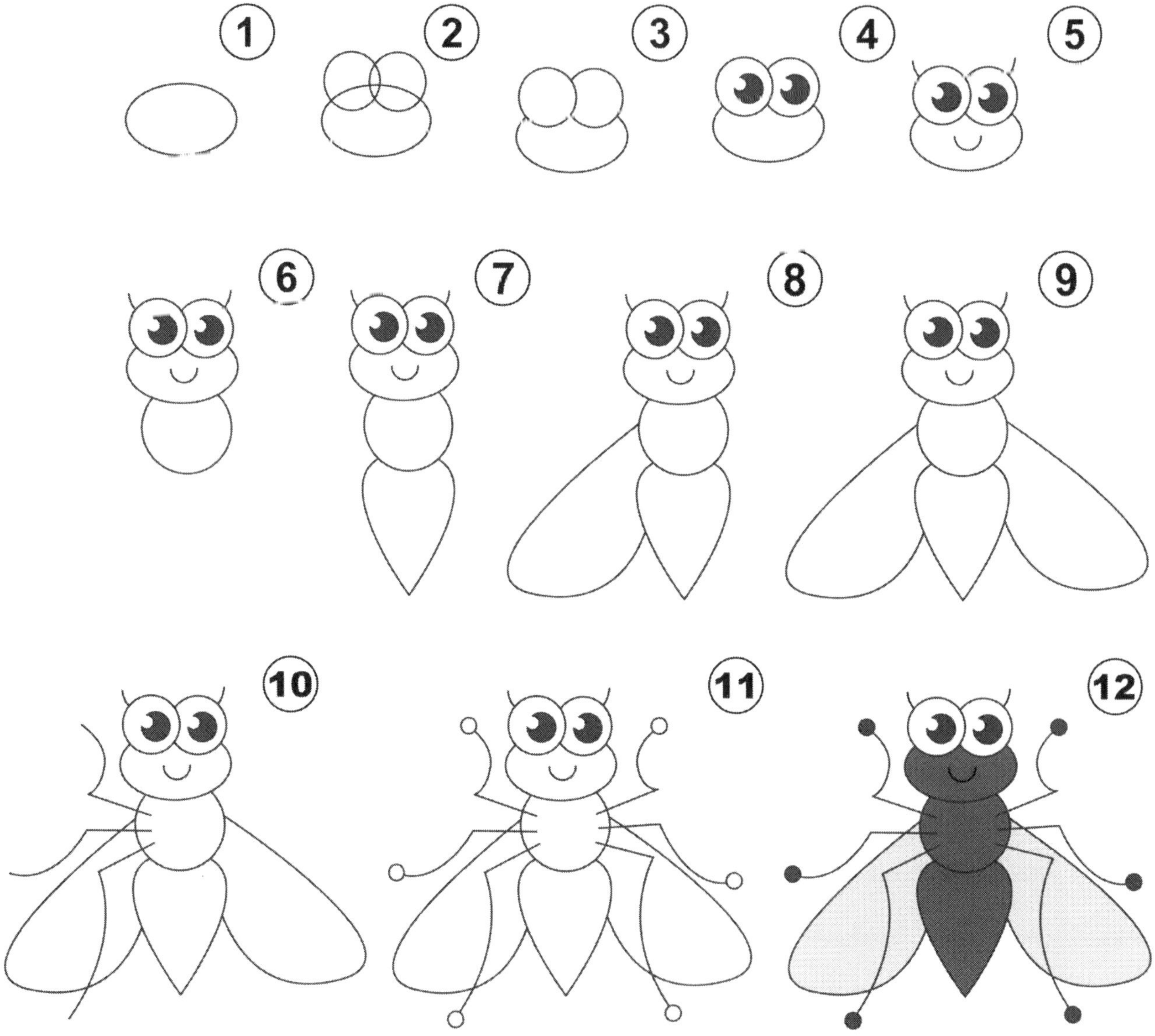
1
2
3
4
5
6
7
8
9
10
11
12

Here you can practice...

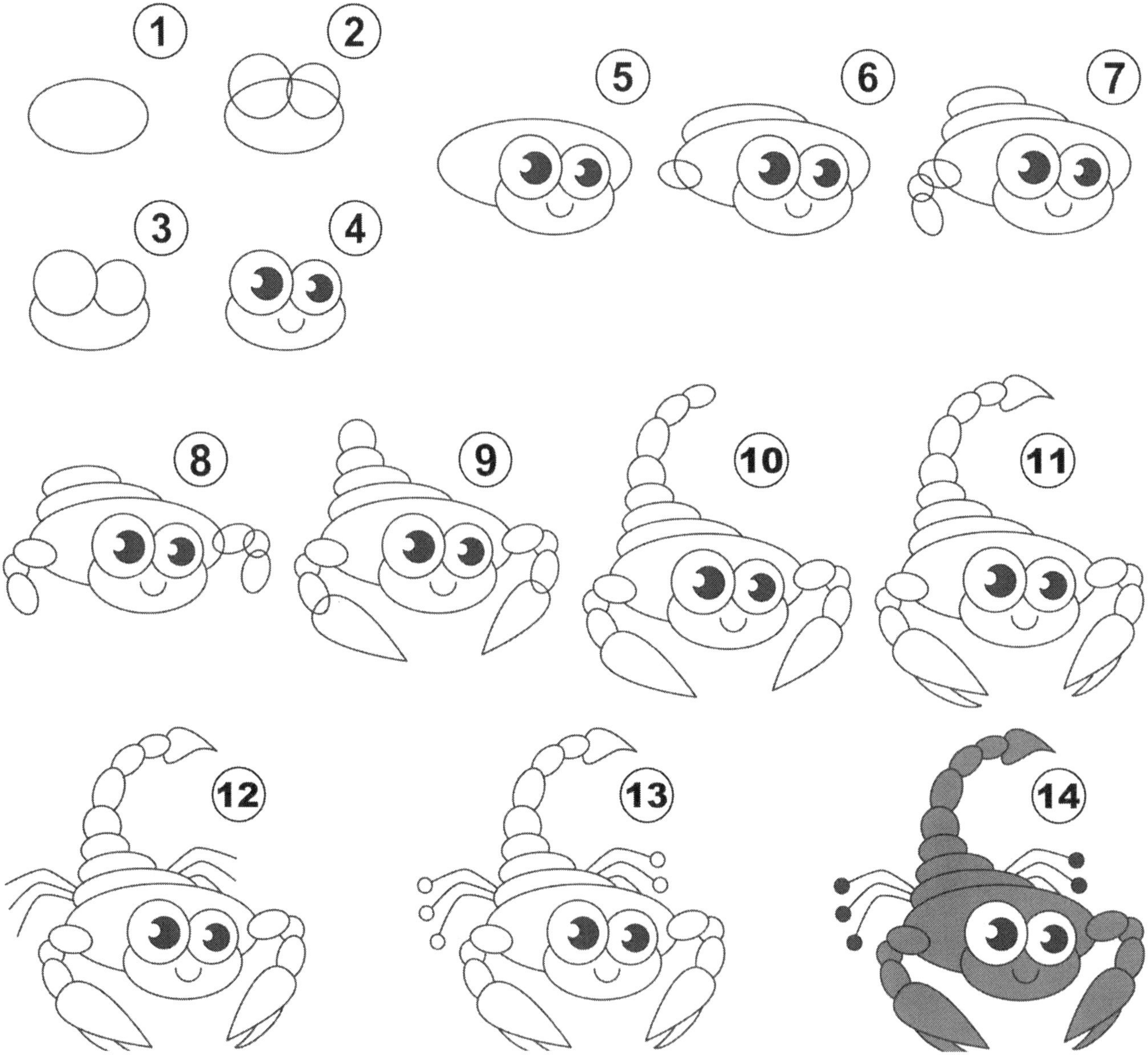
1
2
3
4
5
6
7
8
9
10
11
12
13
14

Here you can practice...

① ② ③ ④ ⑤ ⑥ ⑦ ⑧ ⑨ ⑩ ⑪

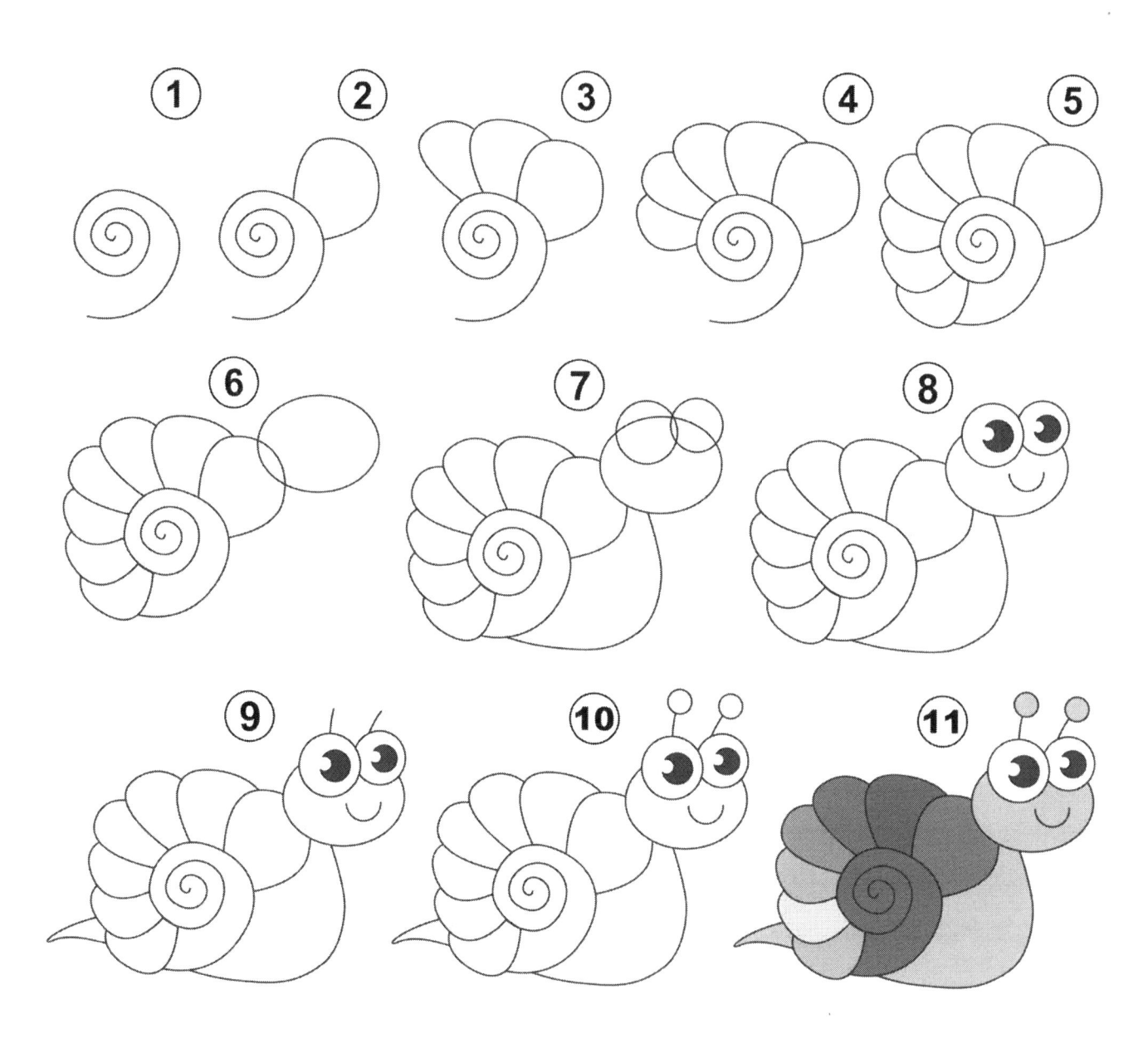

Here you can practice...

1 2 3 4 5 6 7 8 9 10 11 12

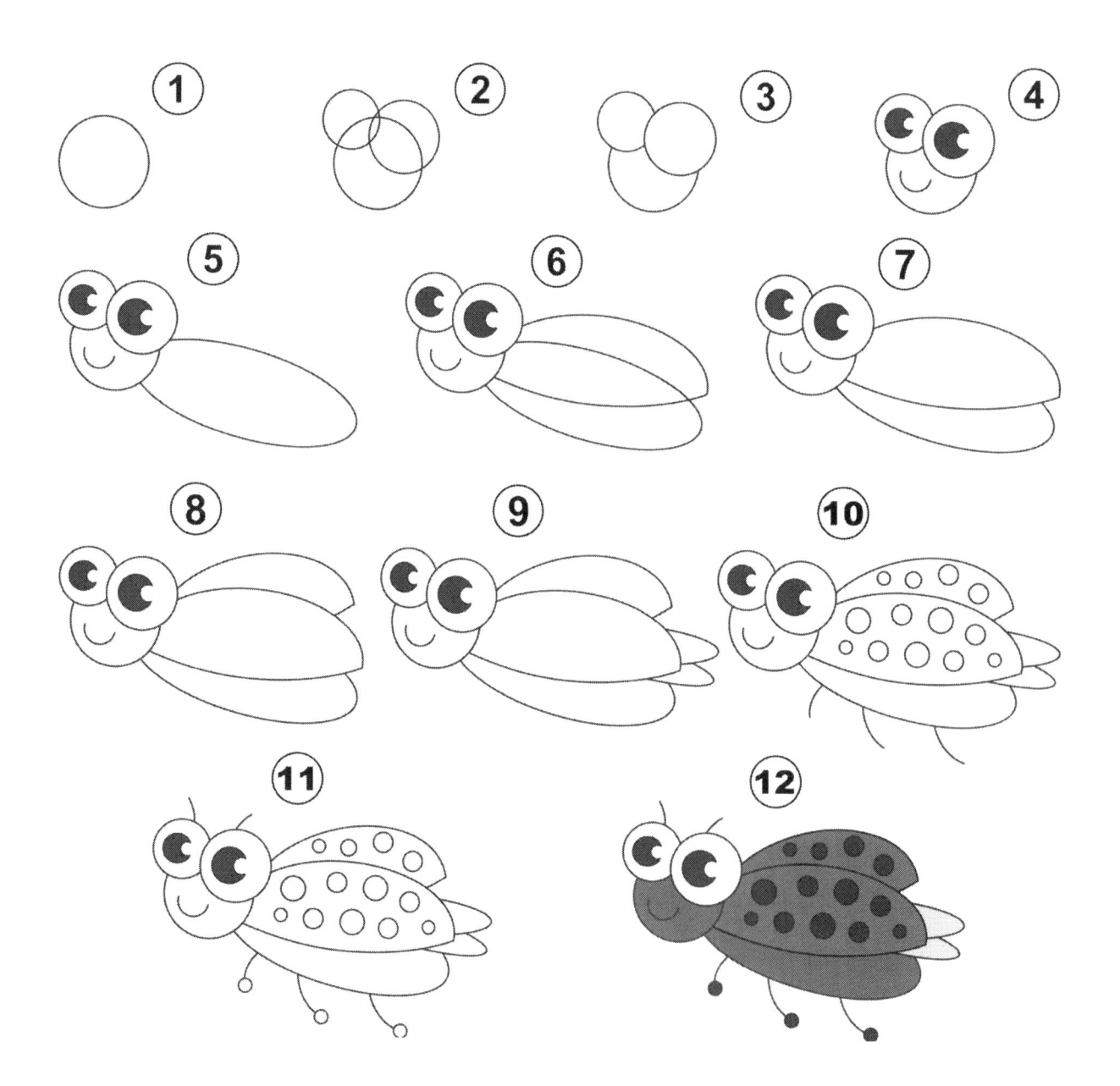

Here you can practice...

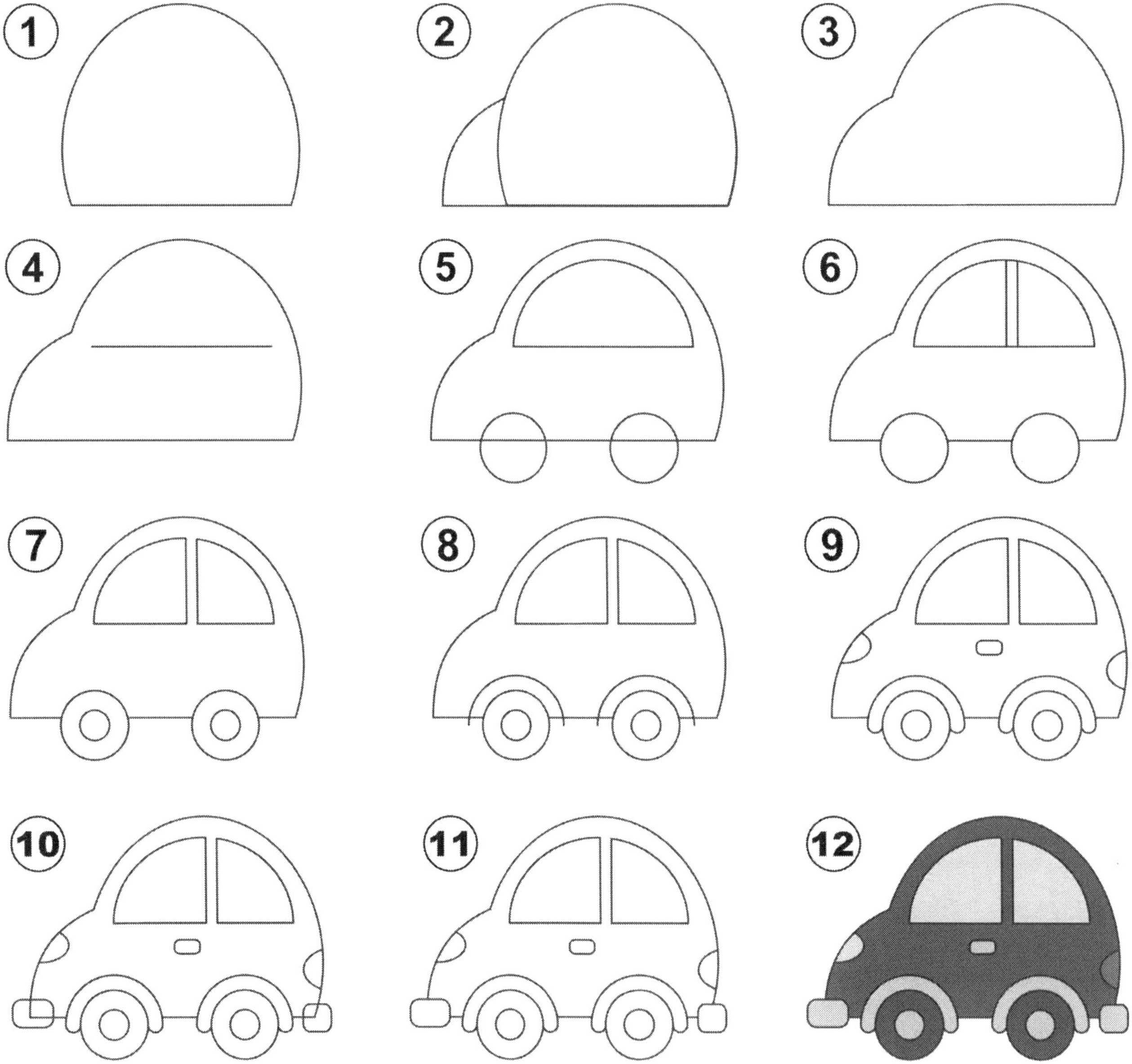
1
2
3
4
5
6
7
8
9
10
11
12

Here you can practice...

① ② ③ ④ ⑤ ⑥ ⑦ ⑧

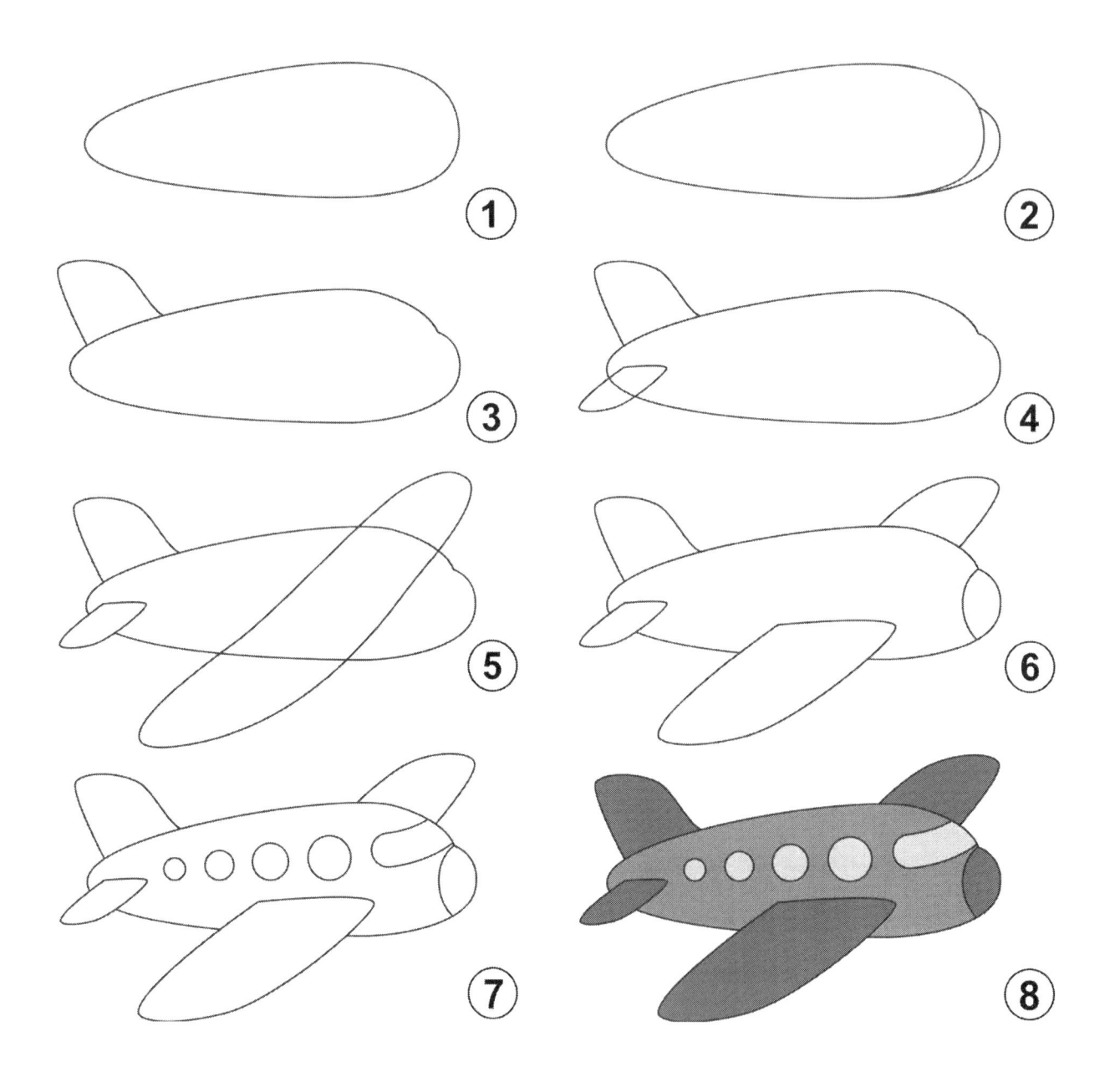

Here you can practice...

① ② ③ ④ ⑤ ⑥ ⑦ ⑧ ⑨ ⑩ ⑪ ⑫ ⑬

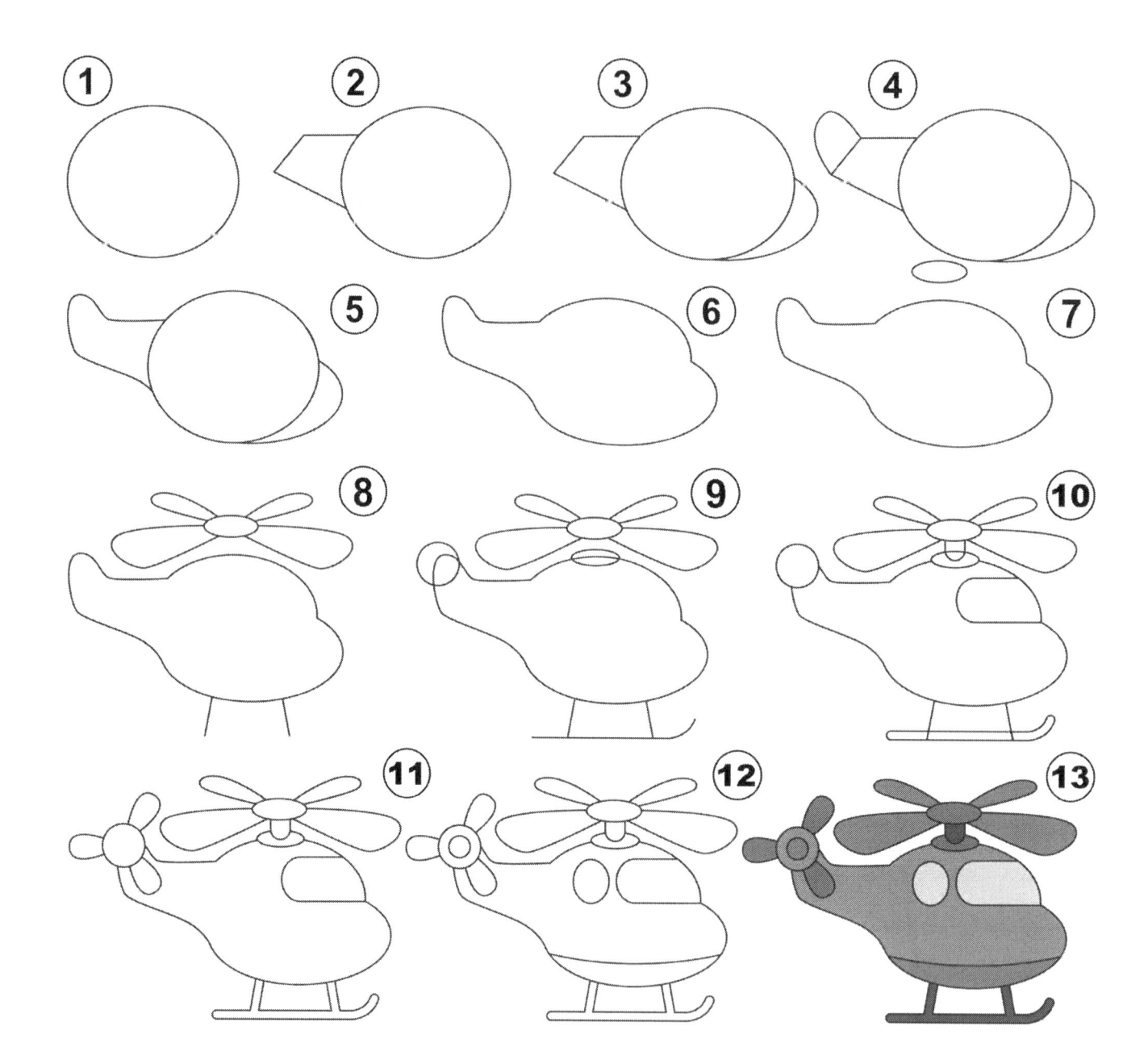

Here you can practice...

Here you can practice...

Here you can practice...

Impressum

© How To Draw For Kids

All rights reserved.

© Pictures:

Kid_Games_Catalog/shutterstock.com

Contact:

Alexander Polupanow

Heinrich-Steul-Str. 21

34123 Kassel

Germany

Alex.polupanow@gmail.com

Made in the USA
Middletown, DE
23 November 2018